My
Hiding
Place

GLORIA K. MWAPE

authorHOUSE®

AuthorHouse™ UK Ltd.
1663 Liberty Drive
Bloomington, IN 47403 USA
www.authorhouse.co.uk
Phone: 0800.197.4150

*Author Credits: Rhonda Byrne the author of the secret who inspired me a lot to always share
love to billions. Graham Cooke, author of developing your prophetic gift, who inspires me
to use my gifts to the benefits of others. Amie Dockery and le Sadhou Sundar Singh.*

*Bible version: NKJV = New King James Version 1982 by Thomas Nelson
King James Bible 2012
Holy Bible, New International Version®, NIV® Copyright © 1973, 1978, 1984, 2011
by Biblica, Inc.® Used by permission. All rights reserved worldwide.*

*Scripture quotations are taken from the Holy Bible, New
Living Translation, copyright ©1996, 2004, 2007.
Used by permission of Tyndale House Publishers, Inc., Carol Stream, Illinois 60188.
All Rights Reserved.*

*King James Bible
Text courtesy of BibleProtector.com
Section Headings Courtesy INT Bible
© 2012, Used by Permission*

Published by AuthorHouse 04/22/2014

*ISBN: 978-1-4969-7827-1 (sc)
ISBN: 978-1-4969-7828-8 (hc)
ISBN: 978-1-4969-7836-3 (e)*

*Any people depicted in stock imagery provided by Thinkstock are models,
and such images are being used for illustrative purposes only.
Certain stock imagery © Thinkstock.*

This book is printed on acid-free paper.

To my late Mother

Agnes,

who not only introduced me to this world

but also taught me to serve God with all that I have

Grateful Acknowledgements

I am very grateful to my dearest father for his continuous support and wisdom.

I am particularly grateful for my first born Elizabeth Davies for her great help that made it possible for me to write this book. I am also grateful to my husband Luke C. Davies for his love and encouragement, to my son David and Emmanuel Davies for their patience and understanding while I spent many hours working on this book, to my young daughter Zepporah Davies for her care and compliment, to my mentor Patching and Eira who taught me to live a life of a slave of Christ. To my co -workers in the ministry Pastor Austin and his wife Annie for their timely encouragement, counsel and suggestions. To my older sister Raphael who led me to Christ. To my friends Anna Leppert for believing in my calling and for her sincere friendship, Sherani and Nivasha Govender for their trust and encouragment when I was feeling exhausted to pursue my dreams, to my good friend Rina Nagel for making me realise the value of the book or my ability to finish it, to Madeleine Maloba for her great seed she sow in my ministry in times of need, to my friend Jolina Mbenga for her prophetic words for this book, to my Eldest sister Vanilla and her husband Kizito for their advise. To Reverend William Mukeba and his wife

Passy Mukeba for allowing me to work on my abilities and serve God together in their church Fountain of Faith that gave me a platform to live every single word I preached in this book. To my cousins Petros and Jose for always keeping in touch with me and keeping track on the work of God and on this book. My special thanks to all the members of Rise Again Ministry for their prayers of intercessions, especially Pichou Tshipadi and and his caring wife Angel, to Dr. Belinda Mwepu and her humble husband Freddy for their financial support. To all of you who corrected me, believed in me and who will read this book, big thanks.

I am also Indebted to Authorhouse publishers for working with me and publishing this book.

Contents

INTRODUCTION

My prayer is that the Almighty God and father of our Lord Jesus Christ, who has blessed us all in the celestial sphere with every spiritual blessing in Christ and has chosen us in him before the creation of the world, will reveal himself in a supernatural way to every reader of this book like he has done with me.

There is enough grace for everybody but not enough time for all. If he didn't do it I would have not done it. A hiding place is a place where you go alone and find refuge from somebody or something. It's a place of romancing with God, a place where you display your true colours. Beyond what you see, God knows what is best for you. Just run to him until you feel or know that you are now safe. Have you ever been in a situation whereby you don't know what to say or do but running away is the only immediate solution? No one will take you there. People can cause and persuade you to go there but you just have to do it alone. When there is no road to get to your heart God will use situations, people that you do not even know and events to lead you to this hiding place. There, you will cry and let go. You will discover the real you. You will surrender and eventually be released to be used by Him tremendously.

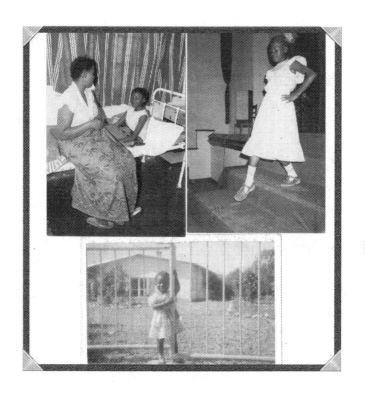

The Little Girl

She was born in Africa in the late years of the 1970's. At the age of two she was already escaping from her house managing to go to the front gate. She would greet every person that passed by till her mother would find her there. She was brought back into the house where her mom would keep her eyes on her for a while. She was the fourth child of six and loved the people, the world and nature. Although she was young she especially loved dangerous places. Usually marked *Do not trespass.*

One morning the whole family went to visit a few relatives in the neighbourhood about 30 km away from where they lived. Excited, she thought of how fun it would be to stand by the side of the road just to see and greet strangers. By then she was six and had convinced herself to believe that she was old enough to handle herself before everybody else. A few hours later they had arrived and settled in. The little girl sneaked out, running off to the gate. There she was busy with strangers. Genuinely, she greeted an old lady with such joy. Rapidly coming close, the old lady opened the flask she had in her hands and poured hot tea on the little ones feet, she began to dream of being a world entertainer just to please everybody. One day she was not afraid to dream out loud, she heard a song playing on the radio and began to dance to it right in front of her parents, her brother and sisters. So pleased with her talent they all encouraged her to join a group of dancers and so thatswhere her fun began. She was 12 when she joined the band *Les Charmeurs*. At that time life presented her with so many talented and wealthy friends who offered to choreograph her. After school she would spend weekends with all those wealthy friends in their luxurious houses for rehearsals. With her founder mental courage she participated in many competitions and became quite famous in the town she was living in. Her fans gave her a nickname *Cathy Katra.* Unexpectedly one of her best friend's parent who was supporting them financially with all the competitions and practices became very sick and died in 1988.

She heard the news and refused to believe it until the day of the funeral. When everyone cried, she took a look at the dead man. He was very generous and she realised that. She wondered how and why it happened. Her family could see the look on her face, that the situation tore her apart. She never thought that it would be a difficult task to achieve her dreams. After some time later they commenced with their practice but the children of the late sponsor were not part of the group any longer. Things became tough but she went on persuading the rest of the group that they could make it without the others. In the middle of the same year the leader of the band came to give his goodbyes. His father who was involved in political affairs had to leave town forever and obviously the band could not cope again. In the meantime she was in grade seven but the results of that term were so bad that her father beat her aggressively out of disappointment for the first and last time. He prohibited her from pursuing her dreams to any further extent. I should mention that Malaria was one of the diseases that the little girl had consistently. After many check ups the doctor admitted her into hospital where she was kept in bed for a week because the malaria was cerebral. Two of her classmates that were ill shared the same room and passed away the very same week.

"What do I do?". She questioned her mother, who was always by her side. "Oh Mama, why is my world crushing down over me?. I know I am next on the dead list", she thought. "When there's no one around me. I can handle that. Being let down. I can handle that. My dreams being shut down. I can handle that. And what about death?, that, I bet I can handle too. She silently cried through the hurts and after she was done she'd cry again. Her mother would convince her that it was for the best but she'd always ask Mama to explain why she was in so many tears?. Mama told her that if she commited herself into the hands of the Almighty God and He would direct her paths. (Proverbs 3:5-6)

She could see that Mama had no solid answer for her. She went through so much as a young girl of twelve. You tell me how could she have ever been normal somehow? Many thoughts came to her mind. "Maybe someone invisible is controlling my life and delaying me from pursuing my dreams. If yes then who could it be and why can't he reveal himself to me?. Why is he not aware of my passions?. Finally she decided not to be concerned about anyone, including herself and anything any longer since she was awfully convinced that nobody cared for her. She turned out negative towards life by always saying her life was not worth living. That little girl put a barrier between the world and herself just so no one could rebuke, influence and teach her anything. Have you ever seen a wild bird feeling sorry for itself?. By now you might wonder what happened next. Who is the little girl?. I am **The Little Girl.**

He Found Me

Long ago the LORD said to Israel: "I have loved you, my people, with an everlasting love. With unfailing love I have drawn you to myself. (Jeremiah 31: 3)

It was the beginning of the year 1989 when I gave up on my dreams of being a world performer. My older sister Raphael was a born again Christian and was involved in the evangelism group. Everyday she would carry her holy book and proclaimed the good news in school during break. I was one of the coolest girls in the school and I once enjoyed performing. So it was kind of embarrassing to watch my sister going on in the same place preaching the gospel of Christ while I was contradicting her beliefs with my life style. I loved the world; I loved everything that was loud and full of life. Indeed I felt I belonged to this big and beautiful world. I would ask her to not come near my friends with her holy book because I was afraid that she might have won them over to Christ and that would have forced me to join her church. Back home in the evening she would call me and gently asked me to give my life to Jesus and to receive him as my Lord and Saviour. I thought if that was important for me? I asked what it meant.

coming Saturday I would go to church with her and give my life to God. During the next week my favourite songs were playing in the bus that used to take us to school, good memories came back to me and so I had seconds thoughts about church. "But I am so young. I want to live a free life. I don't need God after everything he did to me and there is no need to serve him. On that Saturday afternoon, I pretended to be sick. I started to throw myself on the floor in our bedroom holding my stomach and saying that I couldn't walk, that I needed to lay down and that she could go to church without me. My sister Raphael had so much faith in God she asked me to stay on my knees. She wanted to lay her hands upon me to command the sickness to leave my body but I managed to hold her back. I told her it was not good to force me to make a choice when I wasn't that ready. At last she left the room with her holy book. Together with my mother they went to their church.

Late in the evening they came back filled with joy and they were singing praises to God. I envied their joy. It was coming from within them compared to mine. They were happy because they were singing and dancing for God but I had to hear music first then I would feel happy. Clearly I could tell that my joy was coming from outside and not inside me. "All right sister." I said. "Enough with your show off about your joy, I will go with you to the house of your God next Saturday and this time I mean it".

Saturday, the 4th of March 1989 is a day I will never forget. My sister took me to church to receive Jesus Christ as my Lord and personal Saviour. I do not know how I could ever thank her enough for ushering me in the presence of the most understanding and caring being I have ever encountered in my entire life till today. It is not because I was afraid of being condemned by God after death that I had to accept Christ. The day my sister and I entered the church I could hear people making holy noise in that place and they were dancing in such freedom I did not know existed. They were dancing like children. They were never bothered about who was watching. I couldn't make the difference between the adults, the youth and the children. They were all in a circle and were jumping for joy because of their salvation. They were all like brothers and sisters. What a beautiful family it was. I desired to be part of it.

The usher had welcomed me into the house of God with such a warm smile and a holy kiss. I harvest indeed is plenteous, but the labourers are few. Who will hear the calling of God and accept to work for him, to be his mouth, his hands and his feet into this big world?", he asked. With tears on my face I stood up, lifted my hands, lifted my heart, lifted my voice toward the heaven and said "here oh Lord I am, use me for your kingdom's cause". The entire church stretched their hands towards us and prayed for us. The pastor urged the believers to say this prayer after him: **Dear Lord Jesus I recognize before you today that I am a sinner. Please forgive my sins, wash me with your blood and make me holy. Create in me a clean heart and renew a right spirit within me. I believe that you were crucified for me; you rose from the dead to justify me. I receive you in my heart now and I do believe that you are**

my personal saviour. Thank you for everything you have done and are still doing for me. Amen!

Something took place in my heart that day after saying that prayer. Peace overflowed within me. It felt like someone was just waiting to sweep me away in his love when nothing else mattered. The hope which I lost was renewed. The tears that I cried were wiped away. The pain that I used to feel inside me was taken away. I never thought I would find consolation for the pain of being separated from my best friends, my dance sponsor and my classmates who died in 1988. The illness that agonized me for almost three years and the hospital became my home after every 3 months and lastly for my dreams, those I couldn't pursue in the past. I became very confident knowing that someone died for a disappointed little girl like me

Prized Possession

You are the chosen race, the King's priests, the holy nation. God's own people, chosen to proclaim the wonderful acts of God, who called you out of darkness into his marvellous light. At one time you were not God's people, but now you are his people. You did not know God's mercy but now you have received his mercy. (1 Peter 2: 9-10)

When I looked at the way salvation came to me and how Jesus led me into his presence. I asked myself who I was. What humans were that God thought of them; mere mortals that he cared for. The day I received Christ in my life I was given a holy book that became my map till today. As soon as the church service finished, my sister and I rushed home so that I could start reading it before I went to bed. I started with the first chapter of *Genesis,* the story of creation which facilitated me into understanding who I was, where I came from and where I was going. I was so shocked to know that I was created in God's likeness, crowned with glory and honour. He appointed me ruler over everything he made, placed me over all creation. Sheep and cattle, and wild animals too; the birds and the fish and the creatures in the seas. That's every word that God speaks. Within one year I read the whole bible but still wasn't fully satisfied. The truth I discovered was not enough. I needed to personally experience it. It was not the truth that set me free but the knowledge of it. The truth was and will always be there but some remain as atheists because not everyone acknowledges it. I was aware of the truth and its power began to manifest itself by setting me free from any satanic bondage. Sin could not take control over me again. My spiritual eyes were opened, I was able to clearly distinguish the right from wrong. Whenever I did something wrong my conscience would tell me, culpability would weight upon my heart. I was also able to quickly ask God for forgiveness and strength to not commit sin again. Sometimes I would fall into temptation and would forget the words I read in the holy book. I would pray but then I felt like I was just talking to myself. I started to wonder about what was missing in my life.

I accepted Christ as my Lord, I repented, I was baptized in the water and became a believer but why was I feeling so empty inside?. For two years I was living with that emptiness inside of me but still I attended church every weekend, I joined the choir, I took many discipleship courses and I also became an intercessor. I could not afford to miss any retreat, convention and overnight prayers organized by the church, especially when I was hunting for a solution to that emptiness inside of me. Over-night prayers was and still are one of my favourite prayer types that I couldn't miss for anything in the world. The fact that I could deprive myself from sleeping just to spend the whole night in the presence of the Almighty God made me a tough prayer warrior for Christ.

On Saturday the 30th of March 1991, an over-night prayer was organized in the church to prepare ourselves for The Easter celebration. Something supernatural happened to me that night. The pastor of the church was not there but there was another pastor conducting the service. My mother had arranged for so many people to come help her that same night at home with the cooking as she had planned to throw a big party on that Easter Sunday. She insisted on having both my sisters and I at home to also help her with the baking since we were good at that. My heart was very sore to go against her wish for the first time, I had to ask her many times to allow us to participate in the over-night prayer since I had a strong feeling that heart oh Lord, I am waiting for you alone". From my head to my toes I started to feel my temperture rise like fire burning inside of me. I was sweating and trembling. I immediately felt like someone was standing right in front of me. I opened my eyes because I was so curious but couldn't see anybody, I continued to wait upon the Lord then I said, "I know you are here, manifest yourself in me now". With my eyes closed I saw a star shining in front of me. The more I prayed the bigger and brighter it became. It formed into a sun and in the middle of that sun I could see a dove flying down towards me carrying a gold ring on its beak. The dove stopped right before me, above my head it dropped the ring. I quickly lifted up my hands and caught the ring which I thought I would definitely see with my naked eyes. The dove disappeared but the presence of the person in front of me was still there. I had to ask with a loud voice who it was. I heard an audible voice say to me, "**I am your Master, worship me alone**". I replied to him "Master I cannot worship because I honestly don't know how to", and He said to me "You have just been filled with my spirit, now you can worship; call me Jehovah Shammah and I will always hear your voice. I will show myself and answer you. I am not far away from you as you thought I was". (Ezekiel 48:35).

By just being in His presence, reaching His heart and hearing His voice, I felt immense joy in my soul. My inner self was infused with pure love. A mysterious sense of wholeness enveloped me. With humility, I closed my eyes and put my face to the ground in the presence of his majesty, I began to sing a song that I didn't even know. It was a new song of worship that God put on my lips. After midnight the pastor said a prayer and asked everyone to take a break for half an hour but I couldn't hear her, I kept singing. God's spirit caused me to worship till the break was finished. I began to speak in tongues and the pastor was interpreting the message that God was conveying to his people through me. That night, I was filled with the Holy Spirit, whom had given me the gift of comforting, edifying and encouraging.

What a privilege it is to be filled with the spirit of the true God. Forever I will thank him. A vessel that is empty, he will come and fill because he is a generous God. If he could reveal himself to me in a supernatural way, I am very sure he will do the same with you only if you ask him to do so. You might be 55, 34 or even 14 years old and have never heard the voice of God calling you yet you sometimes wonder if he does really speak to people. God is the same God. Our forefathers worshipped the God of Moses, Jacob and Mary and here you have the opportunity to hear his voice through this book. He is speaking to you right now by asking you to not harden your heart but allow him to transform you, to open your eyes so that you may truly see and experience him before it's too late. If you are not yet a believer, know that today as you read this book Jesus is knocking at the door of your heart, he wants you to accept him as your Lord and Saviour and he will fill you with his spirit. Would you open your heart for him?. Know that he crys in secret when he sees you denying him over and over again. Just say yes to him by praying the prayer I prayed and you will start a new life in Christ. Remember, mean it with your entire heart. (ref for that prayer: Chap II: HE FOUND ME)

Looking at what humans do to their fellow brothers, I must mention that it was time for God to come down himself by taking a human nature to rescue all of us from Satan's oppression, to teach us true love and to remind us of where we came from, who we truly are, especially what we were made of. We are the generation of love and we were made of love. You might wonder why it is essential to know him. Well, the answer is obvious. He first created earth for us then he left his glory, his majesty in heaven and came down to seek after you and I. He did not wait for us to draw near to him but he closed himself in frail humanity. He died on the cross naked. He paid the price for our freedom. He became sin (yet he who knew no sin) just so we would be his righteousness. He humbled himself before the people he made. Who would do such things for us, if not our maker?. To the God that you are serving now, what did he do for you? Did he pay any price for you?. It is definitely time that you open your eyes and see that there is a true God who paid the price for your freedom, your liberty before you were even born just to show you how much concern he has for you. Perceive that love is never love until you give it away. Jesus gave himself for you, so turn your eyes upon him and let go of the idols you give excellence to. Do not be impressed with fear, God's arms are always opened. He will not cast you away no matter what you did in your past or even yesterday. Can a mother lose the rememberance of the baby at her breast and have no compassion over the child she has borne?

The Battle Field

In this world you will have trouble but take heart!. I have overcome the world, said Jesus. (John 16: 33)

There is a race that we must all run, there are victories to be won and the world is where this race is taking place. "Let the person who has ears listen to what the Spirit says. I will give some of the hidden manna to everyone who wins the victory. I will also give each person a white stone with a new name written on it, a name that is known only to the person who receives it. I will give the right to eat from the tree of life, which is in the paradise of God", says The Lord. There is a manifestation of favour on the man who undergoes testing because if he has God's approval he will be given the crown of life, which the Lord has said He will give to those who have extending love for Him.

Once being filled with the spirit of God, the passionate emotion that was there was too strong for me to keep quiet about it. The only thing that came to mind was to go out there proclaiming the Good News to the world, not even thinking about the opposition I could face.

On that Easter morning I was indeed comforted by the Shekinah of God. I made a solemn promise that I would teach transgressors the ways of the Lord for the rest of my life and sinners would turn back to him. The very first act of opposition I experienced was with the Senior Pastor of the church where I was associated with. He was away during the time I was filled with the spirit of God. A month before he returned, the Holy spirit spoke to me and commanded me to chose 11 youths within the church and form a group of junior intercessors. The junior pastor was amongst them. The group was called *The Hand of God.* That day when the Spirit spoke to me, I could clearly hear His voice calling me Gloria. I responded to God that my name was Catherine but He insisted and said before the world began I was on His mind and He had called me His servant Gloria, for in me He would display His splendour through His glory and that it would be seen. From then on I was called Gloria and not Catherine. I was very nervous at the fact that when I would explain all this to my parents about why my name was changed, they would not accept it. To my greatest surprise they responded quite positively and told me from the time I was born noticeable changes happened in my family. My Dad experienced a great financial break through right after my birth and the bond between him and my late mother became even stronger. They thought of giving me a name that would remind them of the glory of God after what they had experienced at my birth but they couldn't, so when they heard the news about God changing my name they embraced it with joy and enthusiasm then mentioned the story behind my birth.

The group was completed at that time. We started to preach the gospel of Christ and there were tremendous manifestation of the power of God. People were healed, some gave their life to Jesus Christ and others were set free from demons. As soon as the Senior pastor returned, the members of the church could not wait to meet him and ask about the kind of power and authority we were operating in because our church never experienced that before. He called me in order to test the spirit inside me and I explained everything. Afterwards he called the people who were witnesses the night I was baptized in Spirit to hear if they were able to testify. For 3 days we sought the face of God through fasting and praying together with 4 different pastors from other churches and God confirmed to them that he had set our group apart to bring revival in the church and in the town we were living in. Sadly our Pastor could not stand to see many people healed, delivered, receiving prophetic words and coming to us for encouragement and comfort. From there tension, misunderstanding and jealousy enveloped.

One day the Pastor came to visit my parents to find out if I also prayed for people at home and to his surprise he found nearly twenty people gathered in our lounge praying with us and I was standing in the middle leading them into the presence of God through songs of worship. He had no choice but to sit and pray with us till we finished. After the people left, he called my parents aside and accused me of creating tensions in the church and that I was trying to take his position of Senior pastor. He also prohibited me from going back to his church. My parents were heart broken because they were worried about what would happen to the gift God had given me. I was just a young girl of 15 yet the Lord was using me greatly. So I accepted to stay away from the church, not because I was afraid of the consequences or just to please him but because I was taught to submit to the person in authority.

That day I felt like a sheep without its Shepherd. Doubt started to take place in my heart. I was asking myself questions like why was I cast out of my church and what was to become of me?. I looked at my friends who were not serving God, they seemed to be at peace. I started to wonder why I gave my life to Jesus at such a tender age. Maybe I could have been peaceful like them. "Do I give up on serving God because someone is not happy of what I have become in Christ?", I thought to myself. I remember having many sleepless nights for such a long time. I started to loose my joy of salvation. I couldn't stop praying to God to reveal himself to me once again and confirm my calling. Together with the group we decided to fast for twenty five days. We were sleeping outside the church building without having breakfast or lunch and we were crying out to God. That was my longest fast since I became a child of God. I realised that by fasting I was laying a strong foundation in Jesus Christ the rock of my salvation by going through that rejection. It caused me to draw near to God and to trust him more than anybody in the world. Today I can say that there is no prayer that goes unheard.

A man was passing by my parent's house one day. He decided to come in just to ask for a glass of water. My late mother, being such a good and compassionate woman, welcomed him and offered him something to eat too not even knowing that the man was a prophet of God. As soon as he finished eating he said a prayer for our family and released a special blessing upon all of us in the house. While he was busy praying, the spirit of God came upon him and he began to prophesy over our family. He said to my late mother that two of her daughters that God had set apart for his great commission (he pointed at my sister Raphael and I) are to become servants of God. He said we would certainly go through many trials but God would give us enough grace for each. There would be a time where we would leave the country and go where God will send us just to be tested, corrected, disciplined, purified and established. That confirmation gave me so much confidence that I decided not to ever doubt myself. I realised how precious the gift, the Lord had freely given me, was. I rose again with power and I began to go wherever God would lead me. Be it in a strange family, a school, a church, a market place, a company, or even to a particular person. I accepted to deliver the message from God and teach the word and all that He commanded me to teach. Willingly I chose to serve God and to bow to His will for His glory. Sometimes I would go to certain families where most did not know about the love of God for humanity. I was treated as if I were mad. I faced resistance, opposition and especially humiliation.

A young lady came one day to my place with her eldest sister to ask me if I could pray for them so that they could be rid of an evil spirit that confined them. One of the sisters went on her knees and I prayed for her to be set free. I commanded the demons to leave her, she fell down onto her back and passed out. I kept praying and praying but nothing was happening. All of a sudden her sister was in such panic, saying to me that she would report me

to defend myself against an accusation from that young lady. That time I was living in Zambia in a small town called Ndola. I cried out to God to defend me and to put words in my mouth that I might be able to explain what happened with boldness. I was very terrified of going to jail and to leave my husband alone with my first born child who was only a couple months old by then. After praying the Lord asked me to read Psalm 7 before I left. It is a prayer of David when he was pleading with God for Justice. Obviously David was distressed in this Psalm. He wrote it when he was fleeing Saul's wrath. He puts his case before the Lord, and he believes with his heart that he has not done anything to deserve the ill-treatment from his adversaries. He mentions that if he wasn't the aggressor here, may God bring judgement on his punishment. Of course, he was convinced that he was not wrong and as for me, these words were confirming in advance that victory was on my side. I knew my struggle was not against human components but against rulers, authorities and cosmic powers in the darkness around me.

The police listened to both sides of the story and told the young ladys that they were wasting their time especially because it was firstly a spiritual matter and secondly they did not see anything wrong with whatever I did. We all left the station but they went on saying that they would bring me down in one way or another, I replied that I would not stop what I was doing just because of some sort of fear over what a mortal man can do to me. It's amazing how good God is. He actually allowed salvation to come into the house of that lady two years later when she was involved in an accident after her father got burnt in a fire that was accidently caused in his house by someone and suffered severely in the hospital for many months. She also got divorced from her abusive husband. In the end she came to see me and confessed all the evil plans she and her sister had against the work I was doing for God.

Many years went by and I was still faithfully doing the same thing. Lifting the name of God. One day I asked God why I went through continuous rejection, pain and struggles. Was this the life he had promised to give those who willingly served him?. I was complaining that I could have become a great world entertainer by then, maybe even had more money and became very famous. I was so surprised by God's answer. "For what does a man profit, if he should gain the whole world and suffer the loss of his soul and then what shall a man give in exchange for his soul?, He said.

"I have left everything to follow you!. What then will there be for me?", I replied disappointedly. "Truly at the renewal of all things, when the Son of Man sits on his glorious throne, you who have followed me will also sit on twelve thrones, judging the twelve tribes of Israel. And everyone who has left houses, brothers, sisters, fathers, mothers, wives, children or fields for my sake will receive a hundred times as much and will inherit eternal life", He said back to me. These words gave me even more joy to know that God would never forget anyone who sacrificed his life to follow him and to live by his laws and anyone who accepted to be used by him in order for him to fulfil his purpose in each one of them.

God allows pain in our lives to make us stronger, just like rain is only for a season. What we suffer now is nothing compared to the glory he will reveal to us later. What matters is to understand that earth is just a transit place to heaven. When I was growing up I was taught that life is a journey and not a race but from my personal experience life is a race and not a journey. For if it was a journey we would have just sat, relaxed and enjoyed the ride till the final destination but that is not the case. In order to gain something we must do something. So as long as we are still in this world we should remember that we are situated in **the battle field!**

The Inner Voice

My sheep listen to my voice, I know them, and they follow me: And I give unto them eternal life; and they shall never perish, neither shall any man pluck them out of my hand. My Father, which gave them me, is greater than all; and no man is able to pluck them out of my Father's hand. (John 10: 27-29).

While we are all familiar with our external voices, it is important to know that we also have an internal voice that we have to work with and communicate with daily and that is the voice of God in us. Many people confuse thoughts or passing emotions for this inner prompting of the spirit because that inner voice seems to sound just like theirs. Some call it our conscience, some call it the Holy Spirit or simply God whose purpose it is to offer guidance. This voice has an exceptional power of correction, direction, provision, revelation and transformation. It helps us live the life of our dreams. A beautiful and positive life. It has so much impact on us yet it is just a small gentle sound, a statement, a speech, a declaration, a remark or purely an expression. It can push us into action or inaction as the case may be. This voice wants to help us expand or else we will shrink away from who we are meant to be. Most of us are in control of our lives and end up one day losing everything or even facing premature death. So why can't we allow ourselves to be led by the inner voice?. Those who are led by the Spirit of God are sons of God (Romans 8:14)

The way in which this voice speaks to us is very genuine and straightforward, it can tell you not to go out, to stay home tonight, to pay more attention to what the person in front of you is saying or wake up and pray. I have realized that it is vital to listen to the inner voice and that is why I am writing this book to you, who are reading it now, so you can continue giving ear to your inner voice and enjoy the benefits. If you haven't started listening you can begin to do so now, for the more you don't listen the furthest you are moving from your true path. You will increase obstacles in your paths, you will long for things which you do not have, you will loose your stability and experience a certain emptiness inside of you and in order to not feel like that you will result to alcohol, drugs, cigarettes, sexual immorality or consult people to read your future. You will become a mistake maker. In the end most result to worshiping other gods or even none. Remember that you were granted a free will. Know that your creator wants you to choose to listen to his leading voice inside of you.

Like the psalmist David said : <<The Lord is my shepherd; I shall not want. He makes me lie down in green pastures. He leads me beside still waters. He restores my soul. He leads me in paths of righteousness for his name's sake>>. It was the

One day I was driving home from work, I clearly heard a whisper of one of my closest friend's name. She was by then living in the Democratic Republic of Congo. I looked at my side and there was no one, again I heard a voice mentioning her name. This time I ignored it. After 2 days, in the evening I read my bible before going to bed. Louder than ever I heard a voice calling her name, immediately I said a prayer for her then I fell asleep. Early in the morning as soon as I opened my eyes the first name I heard was hers. I felt the urge to call her but did not know what to say. Eventually I called her, she took long enough to answer, just when I nearly dropped the phone she answered like someone who was in such distress and that gave me more reason to speak to her. I asked how she was doing, she said everything was fine and there am driving, I can't stop in the middle of the road?".

So I drove for almost 5 km and undoubtedly heard "stop" and I got a bit disturbed. It was like the voice was nagging me to stop. Just close to the nursery school where I was going to fetch my three years old son, I saw the stop sign in front of me but because I was speeding and running late, I just passed it. To my surprise a police officer, who was hiding his car beside a tree around a corner, just ordered me to stop and he immediately wrote a fine of a thousand rands. I was so devastated, begging him I explained my reasons of rushing but he still gave me that ticket. Guess what? I arrived so late, the nursery school was already closed and my poor son was the last kid desperately waiting for me with his teacher outside. I was charged with fifty rands for being so late. What frustrated and dessapointed me was having to end the day so unpleasantly. How I wished I had obeyed the voice of Holy Spirit. After finding myself in so many other disturbing and alarming situations I made a decision to listen to my inner voice in order for me to live a fulfilling life. Do you want to be restored and find peace of mind for the rest of your life? Then it is time to listen to **the inner voice.**

Hiding Place

Whom have I in heaven but you? And there is none upon earth that I desire besides you.(Psalm 73: 25)

One day I found myself in a very complicated situation to a point of loosing my job. I was so embarrassed, afraid and unhappy about the situation so I applied for 4 days leave. The people involved in that matter were ungodly. Looking at them, their strengh was firm. I have never seen them in trouble before, they were over confident and possessed more than your heart could wish and were always speaking wickedly concerning christians and less priviledged people. Honestly speaking, their riches always increased and they seemed to be at ease. When I thought of how to understand this, it became too painful for me. I couldn't stop crying on my way home, the only thing I wanted was to hide from my mistakes and to disappear from the face of the earth. You know when you want to do something good for someone and you are being misjudged or misunderstood?, that can take away your confidence and turn you into a negative person. As soon I reached home, parked my car in the garage, I started to question myself, "why me?. Was it it worth it?. Where was

God when I was being mocked or misjudged?. How can he allow that to happen to me?". Not remembering what the scriptures said: **everything good happens for the good of those who love God.** I questioned myself again about why I became a Child of God if I had to always go through such humiliation?

Then with so much anger I said out loud. "God, why can't you take my life away or hide me somewhere until these difficult times are passed away? I hate these feelings so please stop me from feeling like this. Within 4 hours of yearning and praying I felt so strong in my heart that I needed God like never before or a supreme being in whom I could place any reliance excepting God. What about angels or archangels? Can they afford me any support or sustenance, preserve or guide or rescue me from that situation? Should I confide in my closed friend, my parents or my partner? Who on earth can supply me with a substitute for God since he seems so far away from me?"

There are many things on earth desirable as riches, health, friends, sex, food, wine and a lot of other things but not to be compared with the love of God, the grace of Christ, and the communion of the Holy Spirit. There are none to be loved and delighted in as they, nor anything so desirable as fellowship with them. There after my spiritual eyes opened and I could see myself restless searching for a place of safety, for inner strengh and peace. The only thing I was so sure could be good for me was to draw near God and abide in him for he was the only one who could understand me better and confort me because he dwells within my heart. Had

I done so at first I would not have been immersed in such afflictions. The closer you are to God, the less we are affected by the attractions and distractions of earth. Access into the most holy place is a great privilege and a cure for a multitude of ills. This is good and will always be good for me, for you and for everyone to approach God who is the source of good. I suddenly heard deep inside me a question: "Why and where are you hiding?".I then realised that I was hiding from my weaknesses but I didn't have a place where I could really hide. "Should I hide in the house of God where everybody seems content? Should I commit suicide and forget my pains? Should I go to the other continent? What shoud I do? Where is my hiding place?", I shouted.

From that very moment I felt an awesome presence surrounding me, a strong presence I had

I Found Him

"And you will seek Me and find Me, when you search for me with all your heart. I will be found by you says the Lord" (Jeremiah 29: 13-14)

When I was a little girl, I disliked this one game called *Hide and Seek.* My older sister was so good at winning. She would bring her friends, initiate that game then go hide in different places around our big yard. After I would shout, "ready or not here I come" I would hear giggles, but to my concern

I could never distinguish where the sounds came from. I would search once, then sit on a rock saying over and over "here I come!", thinking they would let me find them but they knew exactly how to play the game. Why do you thing I never found them?. It is because my heart was never in the game.

Have you ever gone to church seeking God and instead got the famous words, "If you want to be born again, repent, do good, then tithe"?.Even if you do complete these churchly tasks, does it still leave a hollow place inside of you where you wanted God but were fed religion instead?. Do you ever wonder if there is more to being a Christian than being good and giving money to the church?. Well don't get me wrong. All these things are good and Godly laws to be observed and they definitely lead and show us our way to the Savior. It doesn't save us but it just shows us we need saving. In fact the law was made known to us so we can be aware of sin. Whoever knows what is good and doesn't do it, commits sin.

I am grateful for my hiding place experience as it had set the atmosphere by ushering me in this holy presence of God where I repented, humbled myself, hid my face with my hand to the ground and asked God to forgive my trespasses as I had forgiven those people who trespassed against me in the matter we had at work. I have always known that God existed, thanks to the bible, but I needed my own evidence of a divine being. The bible calls God as the God of Abraham, Isaac and Jacob. I also wanted to have that intimacy, that deep connection with God as Abraham had. So I was open-minded about the supernatural besides the bible. I asked many different people for their personal convictions. I become very active in the church, started to listen to more gospel music. I became a seeker who wanted to find something or someone I could not lose, especially after loosing great friends, the exceptional woman who introduced me to this world who is my dearest late Mother and many opportunities to become a big entertainer in this world.

In that place of confort I released a song of praise and adoration to the heart of God. I gave him my exultation, I poured out my heart till nothing was left. I made my request known to him that I earnestly desired him to be my master forever and to make me more like him by changing me from inside out. My fear was to find myself in another situation just similar or worse than the one I was in before. From there I decided to make time just for him and I. It was kind of a secret place where God and I meet face to face by his grace. It was in my moment of quietness where I was alone and able to worship God for who he is and who he has become to me. He is a closest friend, a lover of my soul, the master of my life and destiny, the answer to my dreams, the solution to all my problems, the reason I live and the God of Gloria. In those moments of expressing my gratitude to Him for everything He had done, He is doing and He will do for me and i was greatful for the great time of worship where I was seeking Him with all my heart, with all my mind and with all my soul that I realised one thing, **I found him.**

Breakfast with God

God you are my God; Early in the morning I will seek you; My soul thirsts for you; My flesh longs for you in a dry and thirsty land where there is no water. (Psalm 63:1)

Imagine a helping hand stretched out to you and yours stretched out for it, together you start to walk harmoniously. Hand in hand like two lovers. As you walk, you notice around you that everybody else is rushing so you decide to let go of that hand and rush as well. Later on you fall you turn around you see the people just watching you then you wonder why couldn't they help me up when I fell?. Have you actually forgotten that you are the one trying to imitate everybody and have you forgotten that you let go of the hand that was there to keep you from falling?

When the sun rises, it's the beginning of a new day. People go to work and perform their jobs till everning. Remember this cliché, *The early bird catches the fattest worm?*. You will hear the birds singing in the branches, the harsh wind that occurs when trains pass at great speed, the buses stopping quickly to fetch a few children attending school and finally you will notice traffic in the most busy roads. Everyone around is showing a great commitment to what they have or love to do because they are fully aware that productive days start with early mornings.

Among these people, you will notice that the majority take breakfast before starting the day. Some successful people who know that time is a precious commodity, invest in family time by having a slow breakfast together where they seize that important moment to dicsuss about family business, expectations for the day, and sometimes laugh, compliment and hope for the best for each other.

Most people know how essential breakfast is and will never allow themselves to skip it for these specifics reasons: For their Memory. Those who had nothing for breakfast underperform on short term memory tests compared to those who'd had their first meal. For their Energy. The longer you go without eating, the more your body starts to slow and shut down. Its doesn't take a genius to glean that food is your body's main source of energy. Without it, thoughts, speech and reaction time sputter and come to a standstill. For their connection. Your brain does a tricky thing when it hasn't had food for many hours, You will start to loose your ability to concentrate. Headaches and hunger pangs will take your focus away from what's really important. Are you going to let that happen to you? For their impulse control. Studies show that when you don't eat breakfast, you tend to look for high calorie, complex-carb snacks against your will because they are fast source of energy and they take less time to break down. For their heart. Researchers have also proven that adults who have a years-long habit of skipping breakfast tend to have higher cholesterol, higher insulin levels. These are all precursors to heart disease and diabetes. Here is the rub. It's not just about eating something, anything shortly after you wake up. It's about eating the right thing.

Now have you heard what the scriptures says: "Man shall not live by bread alone, but by every word that proceed from the mouth of God". If you truly pay attention to these words, you will know that there is no way you can start a day without spending time with God early in the morning. Your Soul cannot talk to you through your own words but communicates through feelings. Therefore feelings are the language of the Soul. At times when you wake up in the morning you might feel empty, depressed, lonely, uncertain, lazy or you can feel blessed, encouraged, peaceful, fulfiled depending on your spiritual level. Understand that just like your body has needs, your Soul as well desires for its needs to be fulfiled.

Through your breakfast with God, you will be able to remember every good thing he has done for you and you will give him your highest praise and adoration. You will be spiritually strong and in control of the day ahead of you. You will become the creator of your day because God's potential to create is now in you, to enable you to create the life of abondance that you deserve. You will start to focus on the good instead of the bad, you will clear your mind and hear him without struggling. You will have dominion over your fleshly desires that might try to lead you in to temptations. At last your heart will be pure and you will begin to see God's manifesting power in your daily life. You will never feel alone because his love will surround you. He will be that helping hand stretched out to you in order to work hand in hand with you. Since God revealed to me the impact of spending time with him early in the morning, I became a happy, confident and peaceful person just because I have started to have **breakfast with God.**

A Life of Contemplation

One thing have I desire of the Lord, that will I seek after; that I may dwell in the house of the Lord all the days long, to behold the beauty of the Lord, and to inquire in his presence. (Psalm 27:4)

I have a little dog named Millanoe. She is a Pug. I used to get so anxious just by looking at her kind and their frightening faces. Now that we own a dog just like that, I became so fond of her. I spent a long time observing her and I saw that she was just another creature who delights living with people. Bit by bit, I begun to see that her face was not scary at all and that she was the cutest dog I had ever seen. Think to yourself, if I had never spent time observing her, would I have been able to see her beauty?.

After finding God, I felt like I had climbed the Himalaya mountain. I decided to never go back to the life of a wandering sheep. Imagine climbing such a high mountain. The amount of energy you spent, the effort you made, the time you invested. You would never let go of that experience for anything or anybody in the world, now would you?. The most important thing or the biggest question is, how does one stay upon this mountain?

I began to search for the purpose of finding an answer. I searched the internet and even prayed earnestly to God to grace me so that I wouldn't go back to the way things were. At times I felt like the beauty of this world would call me to just embrace it, to follow its pattern and live a law-braker's life or live in ignorance of the amazing grace that God has shown by saving a wretch like me, who once was lost and is now found, who once was blind and can now see.

All these experiences are like finding an unusual type of a rose that I can never let it fade or whither by all means. One day in the morning after I heard the birds singing, I decided to join them in declaring the goodness of God through a song. I went outside, placed my camp chair in my little beautiful garden. Gently I lifted up my eyes to the sky, I started to examine it and I realized that all along he was there. Just because we don't really spend sufficient time observing him, we miss out on so many things. Everything that God created was to invite us into a deep relationship through its beauty. All these beautiful things speak to us, to our innermost, far better than anybody intends to. They are silent but they speak. Their mysteries are in that very silence. If you want to understand them you will need to speak their own language which is silence. The Lord God is there through the sun that silently rises in the morning and silently sets in the evenings. He is there through the moon that silently lights up in the night, and He will always be there through the stars that also shine silently in evening.

God has loved us with a love that will never end, just like the sun does not stop rising in the morning so will the love of God toward us. With unfailing love he has drawn us near to himself. In His faithfulness, He devoted Himself to serve us and draw near to us. We can never easily see or hear Him until we look into all that He placed around us with continuous attention. Our mind has to be clear and quiet when we look into His beauty and His perfections. The more we look the more we gain the certitude of God's holy presence and existence.

I could never find the best way to reach out to the heart of God and touch Him like gazing upon Him through His creations. I always feel like He is putting my head on His chest to let me hear His heart bit. This enable me to undertand him, to hear the cry of His heart asking for where will his resting place be since heaven is His throne and earth is His footstool.

Living such a life keeps me fall in love with God over and over again. It like he gets sweeter and sweeter as the days go by. What a wonderful relationship between my Lord and I!

When you fall in love with someone, the first thing that you really want is that it should be forever because the feeling is just so awesome and it makes you feel like you will never fall in love like that again for the person is unique. The second thing is you would love to see that special someone every single day of your life, to communicate with him or her. The last things is you would want to belong to that person and that person to belong to you so that together you share the bliss. The same goes with our maker.

Look how many great things our maker has given us. The greatest gift that He has given to human kind is the gift of love. I am forever grateful for that. Love is not superficial, it is very strong and intense. Love is like the one piece of puzzle that is missing in our world in order for us to have a complete picture. Love is a strong attachement toward someone. God was attached to us from the very beginning when he created the heavens and the earth. Do you now understand why he cannot stop loving you? If you refuse to believe this at least let the nature convince you. From the time a child is conceived the ombilical cord connect the mother to the child. The attachment is established from within the womb. This is how powerful love is.

When we look into God's creations we will discover that they are all telling us a story. Try to look at the sky and examine it, you will see different shapes and colours. At times the sky tell us of the goodness of God and other times it tell us of the greatness of God or the beauty, the power, the tenderness of God. It all depend on what He wants to bring to your awareness.

By observing his works we observe God and by observing God we rediscover our divine beauty. We are all beautiful and perfectly made. The moment we start to spend a significant amount of time gazing into Him and express our deepest gratitude for the gift of life and love, we will establish a kind of special bond between our Great IAm and us. We will be so secure and unshakable for we know his holy presence will never ever live us. We will be his and he will be ours and together we will live in eternity. We will discover more about eternity once we let ourselves live a **life of contemplation.**

Eternal Romance

"For God so loved the world that He gave His only begotten Son, that whoever believes in Him should not perish but have everlasting life. (John 3:16)

Gloria K. Mwape

My Song to thee

From the day you apprehended me

you never stopped thinking of me

You created me in your likeness

to emphasis on our closeness

You gave me what is precious

so that I can remain conscious

You have poured out your admiration to me

because you care so much for me

In your freedom, you let me live

so that I should forever believe

Believe that you are there, always

whenever I strive to discover my ways

The time when I became ungrateful

you showed me how this could be harmful

Because once I desired such liberty

I ended up in poverty

Out of your anger you casted me away from your

   presence

then I realised it was time for me to start using

   my commonsense

How could I ever be so foolish

still you chose for me not to perish

you felt my anguish

you made a way for me to flourish

By giving your only begotten Son

you allowed me to become a new person

This new person now has more opportunities

to live a life where there will be no more

   infidelities

I will finally know a love so pure and beautiful

this love that will be unbreakable and less
painful

This mystery will not be mystery

This mystery will remain history

This history will be our story

Our story that you couldn't stop telling from
the beginning

A beginning that will never have an ending

Once I die in this body, you will welcome me in
your glory

We wiill rejoice forever and ever we will sing a
song of victory

We will live we will love and be ageless

Our romance will be timeless

Let me now exalt your name In expectation of
our **ETERNAL ROMANCE**